THE CHILDREN'S OWN
LONGFELLOW

ILLUSTRATED

HOUGHTON MIFFLIN COMPANY

BOSTON

First published in 1908 by Houghton Mifflin Company

222 Berkeley Street

Boston, Massachusetts 02116

www.houghtonmifflinbooks.com

Book design by Lisa Diercks

Typeset in Bembo

Hardcover ISBN 0-618-11853-5

Paperback ISBN 0-618-11854-3

Printed in the United States of America

KPT 10 9 8 7 6 5 4 3 2 1

PUBLISHER'S NOTE

Longfellow has been fitly called the children's poet. Many of his poems have from their very first appearance been favorites with youthful readers, and for many thousands of children he is the poet best beloved. It has been, therefore, the hope of the publishers that this volume, containing eight of the most popular of these poems, illustrated in color by some of the best known American artists of the present day, will find a ready welcome at the hands of young folks and their parents.

CONTENTS

ILLUSTRATIONS

THE WRECK OF THE HESPERUS

It was the schooner Hesperus,
    That sailed the wintry sea;
And the skipper had taken his little daughtèr,
    To bear him company.

Blue were her eyes as the fairy-flax,
    Her cheeks like the dawn of day,
And her bosom white as the hawthorn buds,
    That ope in the month of May.

The skipper he stood beside the helm,
    His pipe was in his mouth,
And he watched how the veering flaw did blow
    The smoke now West, now South.

Then up and spake an old Sailòr,
    Had sailed to the Spanish Main,
"I pray thee, put into yonder port,
    For I fear a hurricane.

"Last night, the moon had a golden ring,
    And to-night no moon we see!"
The skipper, he blew a whiff from his pipe,
    And a scornful laugh laughed he.

Colder and louder blew the wind,
   A gale from the Northeast,
The snow fell hissing in the brine,
   And the billows frothed like yeast.

Down came the storm, and smote amain
   The vessel in its strength;
She shuddered and paused, like a frighted steed,
   Then leaped her cable's length.

"Come hither! come hither! my little daughtèr,
   And do not tremble so;
For I can weather the roughest gale
   That ever wind did blow."

He wrapped her warm in his seaman's coat
   Against the stinging blast;
He cut a rope from a broken spar,
   And bound her to the mast.

"O father! I hear the church-bells ring,
   Oh say, what may it be?"
"'T is a fog-bell on a rock-bound coast!"—
   And he steered for the open sea.

"O father! I hear the sound of guns,
   Oh say, what may it be?"
"Some ship in distress, that cannot live
   In such an angry sea!"

"O father! I see a gleaming light,
    Oh say, what may it be?"
But the father answered never a word,
    A frozen corpse was he.

Lashed to the helm, all stiff and stark,
    With his face turned to the skies,
The lantern gleamed through the gleaming snow
    On his fixed and glassy eyes.

Then the maiden clasped her hands and prayed
    That saved she might be;
And she thought of Christ, who stilled the wave,
    On the Lake of Galilee.

And fast through the midnight dark and drear,
    Through the whistling sleet and snow,
Like a sheeted ghost, the vessel swept
    Tow'rds the reef of Norman's Woe.

And ever the fitful gusts between
    A sound came from the land;
It was the sound of the trampling surf
    On the rocks and the hard sea-sand.

The breakers were right beneath her bows,
    She drifted a dreary wreck,
And a whooping billow swept the crew
    Like icicles from her deck.

She struck where the white and fleecy waves
    Looked soft as carded wool,
But the cruel rocks, they gored her side
    Like the horns of an angry bull.

Her rattling shrouds, all sheathed in ice,
    With the masts went by the board;
Like a vessel of glass, she stove and sank,
    Ho! ho! the breakers roared!

At daybreak, on the bleak sea-beach,
    A fisherman stood aghast,
To see the form of a maiden fair,
    Lashed close to a drifting mast.

The salt sea was frozen on her breast,
    The salt tears in her eyes;
And he saw her hair, like the brown sea-weed
    On the billows fall and rise.

Such was the wreck of the Hesperus,
    In the midnight and the snow!
Christ save us all from a death like this,
    On the reef of Norman's Woe!

THE VILLAGE BLACKSMITH

Under a spreading chestnut-tree
    The village smithy stands;
The smith, a mighty man is he,
    With large and sinewy hands;
And the muscles of his brawny arms
    Are strong as iron bands.

His hair is crisp, and black, and long,
    His face is like the tan;
His brow is wet with honest sweat,
    He earns whate'er he can,
And looks the whole world in the face,
    For he owes not any man.

Week in, week out, from morn till night,
    You can hear his bellows blow;
You can hear him swing his heavy sledge,
    With measured beat and slow,
Like a sexton ringing the village bell,
    When the evening sun is low.

And children coming home from school
    Look in at the open door;
They love to see the flaming forge,
    And hear the bellows roar,
And catch the burning sparks that fly
    Like chaff from a threshing-floor.

He goes on Sunday to the church,
　And sits among his boys;
He hears the parson pray and preach,
　He hears his daughter's voice,
Singing in the village choir,
　And it makes his heart rejoice.

It sounds to him like her mother's voice,
　Singing in Paradise!
He needs must think of her once more,
　How in the grave she lies;
And with his hard, rough hand he wipes
　A tear out of his eyes.

Toiling, — rejoicing, — sorrowing,
　Onward through life he goes;
Each morning sees some task begin,
　Each evening sees it close;
Something attempted, something done,
　Has earned a night's repose.

Thanks, thanks to thee, my worthy friend,
　For the lesson thou hast taught!
Thus at the flaming forge of life
　Our fortunes must be wrought;
Thus on its sounding anvil shaped
　Each burning deed and thought.

EVANGELINE

This is the forest primeval. The murmuring pines and the
    hemlocks,
Bearded with moss, and in garments green, indistinct in the
    twilight,
Stand like Druids of eld, with voices sad and prophetic,
Stand like harpers hoar, with beards that rest on their
    bosoms.
Loud from its rocky caverns, the deep-voiced neighboring
    ocean
Speaks, and in accents disconsolate answers the wail of the
    forest.

  This is the forest primeval; but where are the hearts that
    beneath it
Leaped like the roe, when he hears in the woodland the
    voice of the huntsman?
Where is the thatch-roofed village, the home of Acadian
    farmers, —
Men whose lives glided on like rivers that water the
    woodlands,
Darkened by shadows of earth, but reflecting an image of
    heaven?
Waste are those pleasant farms, and the farmers forever
    departed!

Scattered like dust and leaves, when the mighty blasts of
    October
Seize them, and whirl them aloft, and sprinkle them far o'er
    the ocean.
Naught but tradition remains of the beautiful village of
    Grand-Pré.

  Ye who believe in affection that hopes, and endures, and is
    patient,
Ye who believe in the beauty and strength of woman's
    devotion,
List to the mournful tradition, still sung by the pines of the
    forest;
List to a Tale of Love in Acadie, home of the happy.

PART THE FIRST

I

In the Acadian land, on the shores of the Basin of Minas,
Distant, secluded, still, the little village of Grand-Pré
Lay in the fruitful valley. Vast meadows stretched to the
      eastward,
Giving the village its name, and pasture to flocks without
      number.
Dikes, that the hands of the farmers had raised with labor
      incessant,
Shut out the turbulent tides; but at stated seasons the flood-
      gates
Opened, and welcomed the sea to wander at will o'er the
      meadows.
West and south there were fields of flax, and orchards and
      cornfields
Spreading afar and unfenced o'er the plain; and away to the
      northward
Blomidon rose, and the forests old, and aloft on the
      mountains
Sea-fogs pitched their tents, and mists from the mighty
      Atlantic
Looked on the happy valley, but ne'er from their station
      descended.
There, in the midst of its farms, reposed the Acadian village.

Strongly built were the houses, with frames of oak and of
    hemlock,
Such as the peasants of Normandy built in the reign of the
    Henries.
Thatched were the roofs, with dormer-windows; and gables
    projecting
Over the basement below protected and shaded the
    doorway.
There in the tranquil evenings of summer, when brightly
    the sunset
Lighted the village street, and gilded the vanes on the
    chimneys,
Matrons and maidens sat in snow-white caps and in kirtles
Scarlet and blue and green, with distaffs spinning the golden
Flax for the gossiping looms, whose noisy shuttles within
    doors
Mingled their sounds with the whir of the wheels and the
    songs of the maidens.
Solemnly down the street came the parish priest, and the
    children
Paused in their play to kiss the hand he extended to bless
    them.
Reverend walked he among them; and up rose matrons and
    maidens,
Hailing his slow approach with words of affectionate
    welcome.
Then came the laborers home from the field, and serenely
    the sun sank
Down to his rest, and twilight prevailed. Anon from the
    belfry

Softly the Angelus sounded, and over the roofs of the village
Columns of pale blue smoke, like clouds of incense
      ascending,
Rose from a hundred hearths, the homes of peace and
      contentment.
Thus dwelt together in love these simple Acadian farmers, —
Dwelt in the love of God and of man. Alike were they free
      from
Fear, that reigns with the tyrant, and envy, the vice of
      republics.
Neither locks had they to their doors, nor bars to their
      windows;
But their dwellings were open as day and the hearts of the
      owners;
There the richest was poor, and the poorest lived in
      abundance.

  Somewhat apart from the village, and nearer the Basin of
      Minas,
Benedict Bellefontaine, the wealthiest farmer of Grand-Pré,
Dwelt on his goodly acres; and with him, directing his
      household,
Gentle Evangeline lived, his child, and the pride of the
      village.
Stalworth and stately in form was the man of seventy
      winters;
Hearty and hale was he, an oak that is covered with snow-
      flakes;
White as the snow were his locks, and his cheeks as brown as
      the oak-leaves.

Fair was she to behold, that maiden of seventeen summers.
Black were her eyes as the berry that grows on the thorn by
      the wayside,
Black, yet how softly they gleamed beneath the brown shade
      of her tresses!
Sweet was her breath as the breath of kine that feed in the
      meadows.
When in the harvest heat she bore to the reapers at noontide
Flagons of home-brewed ale, ah! fair in sooth was the
      maiden.
Fair was she when, on Sunday morn, while the bell from its
      turret
Sprinkled with holy sounds the air, as the priest with his
      hyssop
Sprinkles the congregation, and scatters blessings upon them,
Down the long street she passed, with her chaplet of beads
      and her missal,
Wearing her Norman cap, and her kirtle of blue, and the
      ear-rings,
Brought in the olden time from France, and since, as an
      heirloom,
Handed down from mother to child, through long
      generations.
But a celestial brightness—a more ethereal beauty—
Shone on her face and encircled her form, when, after
      confession,
Homeward serenely she walked with God's benediction
      upon her.
When she had passed, it seemed like the ceasing of exquisite
      music.

Basil was Benedict's friend. Their children from earliest
    childhood
Grew up together as brother and sister; and Father Felician,
Priest and pedagogue both in the village, had taught them
    their letters
Out of the selfsame book, with the hymns of the church
    and the plain-song.
But when the hymn was sung, and the daily lesson
    completed,
Swiftly they hurried away to the forge of Basil the
    blacksmith.
There at the door they stood, with wondering eyes to
    behold him
Take in his leathern lap the hoof of the horse as a play-
    thing,
Nailing the shoe in its place; while near him the tire of the
    cart-wheel
Lay like a fiery snake, coiled round in a circle of cinders.
Oft on autumnal eves, when without in the gathering
    darkness
Bursting with light seemed the smithy, through every cranny
    and crevice,
Warm by the forge within they watched the laboring
    bellows,
And as its panting ceased, and the sparks expired in the ashes,
Merrily laughed, and said they were nuns going into the
    chapel.
Oft on sledges in winter, as swift as the swoop of the eagle,
Down the hillside bounding, they glided away o'er the
    meadow.

Oft in the barns they climbed to the populous nests on the
    rafters,
Seeking with eager eyes that wondrous stone, which the
    swallow
Brings from the shore of the sea to restore the sight of its
    fledglings;
Lucky was he who found that stone in the nest of the
    swallow!
Thus passed a few swift years, and they no longer were
    children.
He was a valiant youth, and his face, like the face of the
    morning,
Gladdened the earth with its light, and ripened thought into
    action.
She was a woman now, with the heart and hopes of a
    woman.
"Sunshine of Saint Eulalie" was she called; for that was the
    sunshine
Which, as the farmers believed, would load their orchards
    with apples;
She, too, would bring to her husband's house delight and
    abundance,
Filling it with love and the ruddy faces of children.

II

Now had the season returned, when the nights grow colder
    and longer,
And the retreating sun the sign of the Scorpion enters.
Birds of passage sailed through the leaden air, from the ice-
    bound,

Desolate northern bays to the shores of tropical islands.
Harvests were gathered in; and wild with the winds of
      September
Wrestled the trees of the forest, as Jacob of old with the
      angel.
All the signs foretold a winter long and inclement.
Bees, with prophetic instinct of want, had hoarded their
      honey
Till the hives overflowed; and the Indian hunters asserted
Cold would the winter be, for thick was the fur of the foxes.
Such was the advent of autumn. Then followed that
      beautiful season,
Called by the pious Acadian peasants the Summer of All-
      Saints!
Filled was the air with a dreamy and magical light; and the
      landscape
Lay as if new-created in all the freshness of childhood.
Peace seemed to reign upon earth, and the restless heart of
      the ocean
Was for a moment consoled. All sounds were in harmony
      blended.
Voices of children at play, the crowing of cocks in the farm-
      yards,
Whir of wings in the drowsy air, and the cooing of pigeons,
All were subdued and low as the murmurs of love, and the
      great sun
Looked with the eye of love through the golden vapors
      around him;
While arrayed in its robes of russet and scarlet and yellow,

Bright with the sheen of the dew, each glittering tree of the
     forest
Flashed like the plane-tree the Persian adorned with mantles
     and jewels.

Now recommenced the reign of rest and affection and
     stillness.
Day with its burden and heat had departed, and twilight
     descending
Brought back the evening star to the sky, and the herds to
     the homestead.
Pawing the ground they came, and resting their necks on
     each other,
And with their nostrils distended inhaling the freshness of
     evening.
Foremost, bearing the bell, Evangeline's beautiful heifer,
Proud of her snow-white hide, and the ribbon that waved
     from her collar,
Quietly paced and slow, as if conscious of human affection.
Then came the shepherd back with his bleating flocks from
     the seaside,
Where was their favorite pasture. Behind them followed the
     watch-dog,
Patient, full of importance, and grand in the pride of his
     instinct,
Walking from side to side with a lordly air, and superbly
Waving his bushy tail, and urging forward the stragglers;
Regent of flocks was he when the shepherd slept; their
     protector,

When from the forest at night, through the starry silence the
    wolves howled.
Late, with the rising moon, returned the wains from the
    marshes,
Laden with briny hay, that filled the air with its odor.
Cheerily neighed the steeds, with dew on their manes and
    their fetlocks,
While aloft on their shoulders the wooden and ponderous
    saddles,
Painted with brilliant dyes, and adorned with tassels of
    crimson,
Nodded in bright array, like hollyhocks heavy with
    blossoms.
Patiently stood the cows meanwhile, and yielded their
    udders
Unto the milkmaid's hand; whilst loud and in regular
    cadence
Into the sounding pails the foaming streamlets descended.
Lowing of cattle and peals of laughter were heard in the
    farm-yard,
Echoed back by the barns. Anon they sank into stillness;
Heavily closed, with a jarring sound, the valves of the barn-
    doors,
Rattled the wooden bars, and all for a season was silent.

   In-doors, warm by the wide-mouthed fireplace, idly the
    farmer
Sat in his elbow-chair and watched how the flames and the
    smoke-wreaths
Struggled together like foes in a burning city. Behind him,

Nodding and mocking along the wall, with gestures
    fantastic,
Darted his own huge shadow, and vanished away into
    darkness.
Faces, clumsily carved in oak, on the back of his arm-chair
Laughed in the flickering light; and the pewter plates on the
    dresser
Caught and reflected the flame, as shields of armies the
    sunshine.
Fragments of song the old man sang, and carols of
    Christmas,
Such as at home, in the olden time, his fathers before him
Sang in their Norman orchards and bright Burgundian
    vineyards.
Close at her father's side was the gentle Evangeline seated,
Spinning flax for the loom, that stood in the corner behind
    her.
Silent awhile were its treadles, at rest was its diligent shuttle,
While the monotonous drone of the wheel, like the drone
    of a bagpipe,
Followed the old man's song and united the fragments
    together.
As in a church, when the chant of the choir at intervals
    ceases,
Footfalls are heard in the aisles, or words of the priest at the
    altar,
So, in each pause of the song, with measured motion the
    clock clicked.

Thus as they sat, there were footsteps heard, and, suddenly
lifted,
Sounded the wooden latch, and the door swung back on its
hinges.
Benedict knew by the hob-nailed shoes it was Basil the
blacksmith,
And by her beating heart Evangeline knew who was with
him.
"Welcome!" the farmer exclaimed, as their footsteps paused
on the threshold,
"Welcome, Basil, my friend! Come, take thy place on the
settle
Close by the chimney-side, which is always empty without
thee;
Take from the shelf overhead thy pipe and the box of
tobacco;
Never so much thyself art thou as when through the curling
Smoke of the pipe or the forge thy friendly and jovial face
gleams
Round and red as the harvest moon through the mist of the
marshes."
Then, with a smile of content, thus answered Basil the
blacksmith,
Taking with easy air the accustomed seat by the fireside:—
"Benedict Bellefontaine, thou hast ever thy jest and thy
ballad!
Ever in cheerfullest mood art thou, when others are filled
with
Gloomy forebodings of ill, and see only ruin before them.

Happy art thou, as if every day thou hadst picked up a
    horseshoe."
Pausing a moment, to take the pipe that Evangeline brought
    him,
And with a coal from the embers had lighted, he slowly
    continued: —
"Four days now are passed since the English ships at their
    anchors
Ride in the Gaspereau's mouth, with their cannon pointed
    against us.
What their design may be is unknown; but all are
    commanded
On the morrow to meet in the church, where his Majesty's
    mandate
Will be proclaimed as law in the land. Alas! in the mean
    time
Many surmises of evil alarm the hearts of the people."
Then made answer the farmer: "Perhaps some friendlier
    purpose
Brings these ships to our shores. Perhaps the harvests in
    England
By untimely rains or untimelier heat have been blighted,
And from our bursting barns they would feed their cattle
    and children."
"Not so thinketh the folk in the village," said, warmly, the
    blacksmith,
Shaking his head, as in doubt; then, heaving a sigh, he
    continued: —
"Louisburg is not forgotten, nor Beau Séjour, nor Port
    Royal.

Many already have fled to the forest, and lurk on its
    outskirts,
Waiting with anxious hearts the dubious fate of tomorrow.
Arms have been taken from us, and warlike weapons of all
    kinds;
Nothing is left but the blacksmith's sledge and the scythe of
    the mower."
Then with a pleasant smile made answer the jovial farmer:—
"Safer are we unarmed, in the midst of our flocks and our
    cornfields,
Safer within these peaceful dikes, besieged by the ocean,
Than our fathers in forts, besieged by the enemy's cannon.
Fear no evil, my friend, and to-night may no shadow of
    sorrow
Fall on this house and hearth; for this is the night of the
    contract.
Built are the house and the barn. The merry lads of the
    village
Strongly have built them and well; and, breaking the glebe
    round about them,
Filled the barn with hay, and the house with food for a
    twelvemonth.
René Leblanc will be here anon, with his papers and
    inkhorn.
Shall we not then be glad, and rejoice in the joy of our
    children?"
As apart by the window she stood, with her hand in her
    lover's,
Blushing Evangeline heard the words that her father had
    spoken,

And, as they died on his lips, the worthy notary entered.

III

Bent like a laboring oar, that toils in the surf of the ocean,
Bent, but not broken, by age was the form of the notary
      public;
Shocks of yellow hair, like the silken floss of the maize, hung
Over his shoulders; his forehead was high; and glasses with
      horn bows
Sat astride on his nose, with a look of wisdom supernal.
Father of twenty children was he, and more than a hundred
Children's children rode on his knee, and heard his great
      watch tick.
Four long years in the times of the war had he languished a
      captive,
Suffering much in an old French fort as the friend of the
      English.
Now, though warier grown, without all guile or suspicion,
Ripe in wisdom was he, but patient, and simple, and
      childlike.
He was beloved by all, and most of all by the children;
For he told them tales of the Loup-garou in the forest,
And of the goblin that came in the night to water the
      horses,
And of the white Létiche, the ghost of a child who
      unchristened
Died, and was doomed to haunt unseen the chambers of
      children;
And how on Christmas eve the oxen talked in the stable,

And how the fever was cured by a spider shut up in a
　　nutshell,
And of the marvellous powers of four-leaved clover and
　　horseshoes,
With whatsoever else was writ in the lore of the village.
Then up rose from his seat by the fireside Basil the
　　blacksmith,
Knocked from his pipe the ashes, and slowly extending his
　　right hand,
"Father Leblanc," he exclaimed, "thou hast heard the talk in
　　the village,
And, perchance, canst tell us some news of these ships and
　　their errand."
Then with modest demeanor made answer the notary
　　public, —
"Gossip enough have I heard, in sooth, yet am never the
　　wiser;
And what their errand may be I know not better than
　　others.
Yet am I not of those who imagine some evil intention
Brings them here, for we are at peace; and why then molest
　　us?"
"God's name!" shouted the hasty and somewhat irascible
　　blacksmith;
"Must we in all things look for the how, and the why, and
　　the wherefore?
Daily injustice is done, and might is the right of the
　　strongest!"
But without heeding his warmth, continued the notary
　　public, —

"Man is unjust, but God is just; and finally justice
Triumphs; and well I remember a story, that often consoled
    me,
When as a captive I lay in the old French fort at Port
    Royal."
This was the old man's favorite tale, and he loved to repeat it
When his neighbors complained that any injustice was done
    them.
"Once in an ancient city, whose name I no longer
    remember,
Raised aloft on a column, a brazen statue of Justice
Stood in the public square, upholding the scales in its left
    hand,
And in its right a sword, as an emblem that justice presided
Over the laws of the land, and the hearts and homes of the
    people.
Even the birds had built their nests in the scales of the
    balance,
Having no fear of the sword that flashed in the sunshine
    above them.
But in the course of time the laws of the land were
    corrupted;
Might took the place of right, and the weak were oppressed,
    and the mighty
Ruled with an iron rod. Then it chanced in a nobleman's
    palace
That a necklace of pearls was lost, and erelong a suspicion
Fell on an orphan girl who lived as a maid in the household.
She, after form of trial condemned to die on the scaffold,
Patiently met her doom at the foot of the statue of Justice.

As to her Father in heaven her innocent spirit ascended,
Lo! o'er the city a tempest rose; and the bolts of the thunder
Smote the statue of bronze, and hurled in wrath from its left
    hand
Down on the pavement below the clattering scales of the
    balance,
And in the hollow thereof was found the nest of a magpie,
Into whose clay-built walls the necklace of pearls was
    inwoven."
Silenced, but not convinced, when the story was ended, the
    blacksmith
Stood like a man who fain would speak, but findeth no
    language;
All his thoughts were congealed into lines on his face, as the
    vapors
Freeze in fantastic shapes on the window-panes in the
    winter.

    Then Evangeline lighted the brazen lamp on the table,
Filled, till it overflowed, the pewter tankard with home-
    brewed
Nut-brown ale, that was famed for its strength in the village
    of Grand-Pré;
While from his pocket the notary drew his papers and
    inkhorn,
Wrote with a steady hand the date and the age of the
    parties,
Naming the dower of the bride in flocks of sheep and in
    cattle.

Orderly all things proceeded, and duly and well were
    completed,
And the great seal of the law was set like a sun on the
    margin.
Then from his leathern pouch the farmer threw on the table
Three times the old man's fee in solid pieces of silver;
And the notary rising, and blessing the bride and the
    bridegroom,
Lifted aloft the tankard of ale and drank to their welfare.
Wiping the foam from his lip, he solemnly bowed and
    departed,
While in silence the others sat and mused by the fireside,
Till Evangeline brought the draught-board out of its corner.
Soon was the game begun. In friendly contention the old
    men
Laughed at each lucky hit, or unsuccessful manœuvre,
Laughed when a man was crowned, or a breach was made in
    the king-row.
Meanwhile apart, in the twilight gloom of a window's
    embrasure,
Sat the lovers, and whispered together, beholding the moon
    rise
Over the pallid sea, and the silvery mists of the meadows.
Silently one by one, in the infinite meadows of heaven,
Blossomed the lovely stars, the forget-me-nots of the angels.

    Thus was the evening passed. Anon the bell from the
    belfry
Rang out the hour of nine, the village curfew, and
    straightway

Rose the guests and departed; and silence reigned in the
  household.
Many a farewell word and sweet good-night on the door-
  step
Lingered long in Evangeline's heart, and filled it with
  gladness.
Carefully then were covered the embers that glowed on the
  hearth-stone,
And on the oaken stairs resounded the tread of the farmer.
Soon with a soundless step the foot of Evangeline followed.
Up the staircase moved a luminous space in the darkness,
Lighted less by the lamp than the shining face of the
  maiden.
Silent she passed the hall, and entered the door of her
  chamber.
Simple that chamber was, with its curtains of white, and its
  clothes-press
Ample and high, on whose spacious shelves were carefully
  folded
Linen and woollen stuffs, by the hand of Evangeline woven.
This was the precious dower she would bring to her
  husband in marriage,
Better than flocks and herds, being proofs of her skill as a
  housewife.
Soon she extinguished her lamp, for the mellow and radiant
  moonlight
Streamed through the windows, and lighted the room, till
  the heart of the maiden
Swelled and obeyed its power, like the tremulous tides of the
  ocean.

Ah! she was fair, exceeding fair to behold, as she stood with
Naked snow-white feet on the gleaming floor of her
    chamber!
Little she dreamed that below, among the trees of the
    orchard,
Waited her lover and watched for the gleam of her lamp
    and her shadow.
Yet were her thoughts of him, and at times a feeling of
    sadness
Passed o'er her soul, as the sailing shade of clouds in the
    moonlight
Flitted across the floor and darkened the room for a
    moment.
And, as she gazed from the window, she saw serenely the
    moon pass
Forth from the folds of a cloud, and one star follow her
    footsteps,
As out of Abraham's tent young Ishmael wandered with
    Hagar!

IV

Pleasantly rose next morn the sun on the village of Grand-
    Pré.
Pleasantly gleamed in the soft, sweet air the Basin of Minas,
Where the ships, with their wavering shadows, were riding at
    anchor.
Life had long been astir in the village, and clamorous labor
Knocked with its hundred hands at the golden gates of the
    morning.

Now from the country around, from the farms and
    neighboring hamlets,
Came in their holiday dresses the blithe Acadian peasants.
Many a glad good-morrow and jocund laugh from the
    young folk
Made the bright air brighter, as up from the numerous
    meadows,
Where no path could be seen but the track of wheels in
    the greensward,
Group after group appeared, and joined, or passed on the
    highway.
Long ere noon, in the village all sounds of labor were
    silenced.
Thronged were the streets with people; and noisy groups
    at the house-doors
Sat in the cheerful sun, and rejoiced and gossiped together.
Every house was an inn, where all were welcomed and
    feasted;
For with this simple people, who lived like brothers
    together,
All things were held in common, and what one had was
    another's.
Yet under Benedict's roof hospitality seemed more
    abundant:
For Evangeline stood among the guests of her father;
Bright was her face with smiles, and words of welcome
    and gladness
Fell from her beautiful lips, and blessed the cup as she
    gave it.

Under the open sky, in the odorous air of the orchard,
Stript of its golden fruit, was spread the feast of betrothal.
There in the shade of the porch were the priest and the
notary seated;
There good Benedict sat, and sturdy Basil the blacksmith.
Not far withdrawn from these, by the cider-press and the
beehives,
Michael the fiddler was placed, with the gayest of hearts and
of waistcoats.
Shadow and light from the leaves alternately played on his
snow-white
Hair, as it waved in the wind; and the jolly face of the fiddler
Glowed like a living coal when the ashes are blown from the
embers.
Gayly the old man sang to the vibrant sound of his fiddle,
Tous les Bourgeois de Chartres, and *Le Carillon de Dunquerque,*
And anon with his wooden shoes beat time to the music.
Merrily, merrily whirled the wheels of the dizzying dances
Under the orchard-trees and down the path to the meadows;
Old folk and young together, and children mingled among
them.
Fairest of all the maids was Evangeline, Benedict's daughter!
Noblest of all the youths was Gabriel, son of the blacksmith!

So passed the morning away. And lo! with a summons
sonorous
Sounded the bell from its tower, and over the meadows a
drum beat.
Thronged erelong was the church with men. Without, in
the churchyard,

Waited the women. They stood by the graves, and hung on
    the headstones
Garlands of autumn-leaves and evergreens fresh from the
    forest.
Then came the guard from the ships, and marching proudly
    among them
Entered the sacred portal. With loud and dissonant clangor
Echoed the sound of their brazen drums from ceiling and
    casement, —
Echoed a moment only, and slowly the ponderous portal
Closed, and in silence the crowd awaited the will of the
    soldiers.
Then uprose their commander, and spake from the steps of
    the altar,
Holding aloft in his hands, with its seals, the royal
    commission.
"You are convened this day," he said, "by his Majesty's orders.
Clement and kind has he been; but how you have answered
    his kindness,
Let your own hearts reply! To my natural make and my
    temper
Painful the task is I do, which to you I know must be
    grievous.
Yet must I bow and obey, and deliver the will of our
    monarch;
Namely, that all your lands, and dwellings, and cattle of all
    kinds
Forfeited be to the crown; and that you yourselves from this
    province

Be transported to other lands. God grant you may dwell
    there
Ever as faithful subjects, a happy and peaceable people!
Prisoners now I declare you; for such is his Majesty's
    pleasure!"
As, when the air is serene in sultry solstice of summer,
Suddenly gathers a storm, and the deadly sling of the
    hailstones
Beats down the farmer's corn in the field and shatters his
    windows,
Hiding the sun, and strewing the ground with thatch from
    the house-roofs,
Bellowing fly the herds, and seek to break their enclosures;
So on the hearts of the people descended the words of the
    speaker.
Silent a moment they stood in speechless wonder, and then
    rose
Louder and ever louder a wail of sorrow and anger,
And, by one impulse moved, they madly rushed to the door-
    way.
Vain was the hope of escape; and cries and fierce
    imprecations
Rang through the house of prayer; and high o'er the heads
    of the others
Rose, with his arms uplifted, the figure of Basil the
    blacksmith,
As, on a stormy sea, a spar is tossed by the billows.
Flushed was his face and distorted with passion; and wildly
    he shouted, —

"Down with the tyrants of England! we never have sworn
    them allegiance!
Death to these foreign soldiers, who seize on our homes and
    our harvests!"
More he fain would have said, but the merciless hand of a
    soldier
Smote him upon the mouth, and dragged him down to the
    pavement.

In the midst of the strife and tumult of angry contention,
Lo! the door of the chancel opened, and Father Felician
Entered, with serious mien, and ascended the steps of the
    altar.
Raising his reverend hand, with a gesture he awed into
    silence
All that clamorous throng; and thus he spake to his people;
Deep were his tones and solemn; in accents measured and
    mournful
Spake he, as, after the tocsin's alarum, distinctly the clock
    strikes.
"What is this that ye do, my children? what madness has
    seized you?
Forty years of my life have I labored among you, and taught
    you,
Not in word alone, but in deed, to love one another!
Is this the fruit of my toils, of my vigils and prayers and
    privations?
Have you so soon forgotten all lessons of love and
    forgiveness?

This is the house of the Prince of Peace, and would you
      profane it
Thus with violent deeds and hearts overflowing with hatred?
Lo! where the crucified Christ from his cross is gazing upon
      you!
See! in those sorrowful eyes what meekness and holy
      compassion!
Hark! how those lips still repeat the prayer, 'O Father, forgive
      them!'
Let us repeat that prayer in the hour when the wicked assail
      us,
Let us repeat it now, and say, 'O Father, forgive them!'"
Few were his words of rebuke, but deep in the hearts of his
      people
Sank they, and sobs of contrition succeeded the passionate
      outbreak,
While they repeated his prayer, and said, "O Father, forgive
      them!"

    Then came the evening service. The tapers gleamed from
      the altar.
Fervent and deep was the voice of the priest, and the people
      responded,
Not with their lips alone, but their hearts; and the Ave Maria
Sang they, and fell on their knees, and their souls, with
      devotion translated,
Rose on the ardor of prayer, like Elijah ascending to heaven.
    Meanwhile had spread in the village the tidings of ill, and
      on all sides

Wandered, wailing, from house to house the women and
    children.
Long at her father's door Evangeline stood, with her right
    hand
Shielding her eyes from the level rays of the sun, that,
    descending,
Lighted the village street with mysterious splendor, and
    roofed each
Peasant's cottage with golden thatch, and emblazoned its
    windows.
Long within had been spread the snow-white cloth on the
    table;
There stood the wheaten loaf, and the honey fragrant with
    wild-flowers;
There stood the tankard of ale, and the cheese fresh brought
    from the dairy,
And, at the head of the board, the great arm-chair of the
    farmer.
Thus did Evangeline wait at her father's door, as the sunset
Threw the long shadows of trees o'er the broad ambrosial
    meadows.
Ah! on her spirit within a deeper shadow had fallen,
And from the fields of her soul a fragrance celestial
    ascended, —
Charity, meekness, love, and hope, and forgiveness, and
    patience!
Then, all-forgetful of self, she wandered into the village,
Cheering with looks and words the mournful hearts of the
    women,

As o'er the darkening fields with lingering steps they
　　departed,
Urged by their household cares, and the weary feet of their
　　children.
Down sank the great red sun, and in golden, glimmering
　　vapors
Veiled the light of his face, like the Prophet descending from
　　Sinai.
Sweetly over the village the bell of the Angelus sounded.

　　Meanwhile, amid the gloom, by the church Evangeline
　　lingered.
All was silent within; and in vain at the door and the
　　windows
Stood she, and listened and looked, till, overcome by
　　emotion,
"Gabriel!" cried she aloud with tremulous voice; but no
　　answer
Came from the graves of the dead, nor the gloomier grave
　　of the living.
Slowly at length she returned to the tenantless house of her
　　father.
Smouldered the fire on the hearth, on the board was the
　　supper untasted,
Empty and drear was each room, and haunted with
　　phantoms of terror.
Sadly echoed her step on the stair and the floor of her
　　chamber.
In the dead of the night she heard the disconsolate rain fall

Loud on the withered leaves of the sycamore-tree by the
      window.
Keenly the lightning flashed; and the voice of the echoing
      thunder
Told her that God was in heaven, and governed the world he
      created!
Then she remembered the tale she had heard of the justice
      of Heaven;
Soothed was her troubled soul, and she peacefully slumbered
      till morning.

V

Four times the sun had risen and set; and now on the fifth
      day
Cheerily called the cock to the sleeping maids of the farm-
      house.
Soon o'er the yellow fields, in silent and mournful
      procession,
Came from the neighboring hamlets and farms the Acadian
      women,
Driving in ponderous wains their household goods to the
      sea-shore,
Pausing and looking back to gaze once more on their
      dwellings,
Ere they were shut from sight by the winding road and the
      woodland.
Close at their sides their children ran, and urged on the
      oxen,
While in their little hands they clasped some fragments of
      playthings.

Thus to the Gaspereau's mouth they hurried; and there on
    the sea-beach
Piled in confusion lay the household goods of the peasants.
All day long between the shore and the ships did the boats
    ply;
All day long the wains came laboring down from the village.
Late in the afternoon, when the sun was near to his setting,
Echoed far o'er the fields came the roll of drums from the
    churchyard.
Thither the women and children thronged. On a sudden the
    church-doors
Opened, and forth came the guard, and marching in gloomy
    procession
Followed the long-imprisoned, but patient, Acadian farmers.
Even as pilgrims, who journey afar from their homes and
    their country,
Sing as they go, and in singing forget they are weary and
    wayworn,
So with songs on their lips the Acadian peasants descended
Down from the church to the shore, amid their wives and
    their daughters.
Foremost the young men came; and, raising together their
    voices,
Sang with tremulous lips a chant of the Catholic
    Missions: —
"Sacred heart of the Saviour! O inexhaustible fountain!
Fill our hearts this day with strength and submission and
    patience!"

Then the old men, as they marched, and the women that
     stood by the wayside
Joined in the sacred psalm, and the birds in the sunshine
     above them
Mingled their notes therewith, like voices of spirits departed.

   Half-way down to the shore Evangeline waited in silence,
Not overcome with grief, but strong in the hour of
     affliction, —
Calmly and sadly she waited, until the procession approached
     her,
And she beheld the face of Gabriel pale with emotion.
Tears then filled her eyes, and, eagerly running to meet him,
Clasped she his hands, and laid her head on his shoulder, and
     whispered, —
"Gabriel! be of good cheer! for if we love one another
Nothing, in truth, can harm us, whatever mischances may
     happen!"
Smiling she spake these words; then suddenly paused, for her
     father
Saw she slowly advancing. Alas! how changed was his aspect!
Gone was the glow from his cheek, and the fire from his eye,
     and his footstep
Heavier seemed with the weight of the heavy heart in his
     bosom.
But with a smile and a sigh, she clasped his neck and
     embraced him,
Speaking words of endearment where words of comfort
     availed not.

Thus to the Gaspereau's mouth moved on that mournful
    procession.

There disorder prevailed, and the tumult and stir of
    embarking.
Busily plied the freighted boats; and in the confusion
Wives were torn from their husbands, and mothers, too late,
    saw their children
Left on the land, extending their arms, with wildest
    entreaties.
So unto separate ships were Basil and Gabriel carried,
While in despair on the shore Evangeline stood with her
    father.
Half the task was not done when the sun went down, and
    the twilight
Deepened and darkened around; and in haste the refluent
    ocean
Fled away from the shore, and left the line of the sand-beach
Covered with waifs of the tide, with kelp and the slippery
    sea-weed.
Farther back in the midst of the household goods and the
    wagons,
Like to a gypsy camp, or a leaguer after a battle,
All escape cut off by the sea, and the sentinels near them,
Lay encamped for the night the houseless Acadian farmers.
Back to its nethermost caves retreated the bellowing ocean,
Dragging adown the beach the rattling pebbles, and leaving
Inland and far up the shore the stranded boats of the sailors.
Then, as the night descended, the herds returned from their
    pastures;

Sweet was the moist still air with the odor of milk from
      their udders;
Lowing they waited, and long, at the well-known bars of the
      farm-yard, —
Waited and looked in vain for the voice and the hand of the
      milk-maid.
Silence reigned in the streets; from the church no Angelus
      sounded,
Rose no smoke from the roofs, and gleamed no lights from
      the windows.

But on the shores meanwhile the evening fires had been
      kindled,
Built of the drift-wood thrown on the sands from wrecks in
      the tempest.
Round them shapes of gloom and sorrowful faces were
      gathered,
Voices of women were heard, and of men, and the crying of
      children.
Onward from fire to fire, as from hearth to hearth in his
      parish,
Wandered the faithful priest, consoling and blessing and
      cheering,
Like unto shipwrecked Paul on Melita's desolate sea-shore.
Thus he approached the place where Evangeline sat with her
      father,
And in the flickering light beheld the face of the old man,
Haggard and hollow and wan, and without either thought or
      emotion,

E'en as the face of a clock from which the hands have been
taken.

Vainly Evangeline strove with words and caresses to cheer
him,

Vainly offered him food; yet he moved not, he looked not,
he spake not,

But, with a vacant stare, ever gazed at the flickering fire-
light.

"*Benedicite!*" murmured the priest, in tones of compassion.

More he fain would have said, but his heart was full, and his
accents

Faltered and paused on his lips, as the feet of a child on a
threshold,

Hushed by the scene he beholds, and the awful presence of
sorrow.

Silently, therefore, he laid his hand on the head of the
maiden,

Raising his tearful eyes to the silent stars that above them

Moved on their way, unperturbed by the wrongs and
sorrows of mortals.

Then sat he down at her side, and they wept together in
silence.

Suddenly rose from the south a light, as in autumn the
blood-red

Moon climbs the crystal walls of heaven, and o'er the
horizon

Titan-like stretches its hundred hands upon mountain and
meadow,

Seizing the rocks and the rivers and piling huge shadows
    together.
Broader and ever broader it gleamed on the roofs of the
    village,
Gleamed on the sky and sea, and the ships that lay in the
    roadstead.
Columns of shining smoke uprose, and flashes of flame were
Thrust through their folds and withdrawn, like the quivering
    hands of a martyr.
Then as the wind seized the gleeds and the burning thatch,
    and, uplifting,
Whirled them aloft through the air, at once from a hundred
    house-tops
Started the sheeted smoke with flashes of flame
    intermingled.

   These things beheld in dismay the crowd on the shore
    and on shipboard.
Speechless at first they stood, then cried aloud in their
    anguish,
"We shall behold no more our homes in the village of
    Grand-Pré!"
Loud on a sudden the cocks began to crow in the farm-yards,
Thinking the day had dawned; and anon the lowing of cattle
Came on the evening breeze, by the barking of dogs
    interrupted.
Then rose a sound of dread, such as startles the sleeping
    encampments
Far in the western prairies or forests that skirt the Nebraska,

When the wild horses affrighted sweep by with the speed of
    the whirlwind,
Or the loud bellowing herds of buffaloes rush to the river.
Such was the sound that arose on the night, as the herds and
    the horses
Broke through their folds and fences, and madly rushed o'er
    the meadows.

Overwhelmed with the sight, yet speechless, the priest and
    the maiden
Gazed on the scene of terror that reddened and widened
    before them;
And as they turned at length to speak to their silent
    companion,
Lo! from his seat he had fallen, and stretched abroad on the
    sea-shore
Motionless lay his form, from which the soul had departed.
Slowly the priest uplifted the lifeless head, and the maiden
Knelt at her father's side, and wailed aloud in her terror.
Then in a swoon she sank, and lay with her head on his
    bosom.
Through the long night she lay in deep, oblivious slumber;
And when she awoke from the trance, she beheld a
    multitude near her.
Faces of friends she beheld, that were mournfully gazing
    upon her,
Pallid, with tearful eyes, and looks of saddest compassion.
Still the blaze of the burning village illumined the landscape,
Reddened the sky overhead, and gleamed on the faces
    around her,

And like the day of doom it seemed to her wavering senses.
Then a familiar voice she heard, as it said to the people, —
"Let us bury him here by the sea. When a happier season
Brings us again to our homes from the unknown land of
    our exile,
Then shall his sacred dust be piously laid in the churchyard."
Such were the words of the priest. And there in haste by the
    sea-side,
Having the glare of the burning village for funeral torches,
But without bell or book, they buried the farmer of Grand-
    Pré.
And as the voice of the priest repeated the service of
    sorrow,
Lo! with a mournful sound, like the voice of a vast
    congregation,
Solemnly answered the sea, and mingled its roar with the
    dirges.
'T was the returning tide, that afar from the waste of the
    ocean,
With the first dawn of the day, came heaving and hurrying
    landward.
Then recommenced once more the stir and noise of
    embarking;
And with the ebb of the tide the ships sailed out of the
    harbor,
Leaving behind them the dead on the shore, and the village
    in ruins.

THE SONG OF HIAWATHA

HIAWATHA'S SAILING

"Give me of your bark, O Birch-tree!
Of your yellow bark, O Birch-tree!
Growing by the rushing river,
Tall and stately in the valley!
I a light canoe will build me,
Build a swift Cheemaun for sailing,
That shall float upon the river,
Like a yellow leaf in Autumn,
Like a yellow water-lily!
  "Lay aside your cloak, O Birch-tree!
Lay aside your white-skin wrapper,
For the Summer-time is coming,
And the sun is warm in heaven,
And you need no white-skin wrapper!"
  Thus aloud cried Hiawatha
In the solitary forest,
By the rushing Taquamenaw,
When the birds were singing gayly,
In the Moon of Leaves were singing,
And the sun, from sleep awaking,
Started up and said, "Behold me!
Geezis, the great Sun, behold me!"
  And the tree with all its branches

Rustled in the breeze of morning,
Saying, with a sigh of patience,
"Take my cloak, O Hiawatha!"
    With his knife the tree he girdled;
Just beneath its lowest branches,
Just above the roots, he cut it,
Till the sap came oozing outward;
Down the trunk, from top to bottom,
Sheer he cleft the bark asunder,
With a wooden wedge he raised it,
Stripped it from the trunk unbroken.
    "Give me of your boughs, O Cedar!
Of your strong and pliant branches,
My canoe to make more steady,
Make more strong and firm beneath me!"
    Through the summit of the Cedar
Went a sound, a cry of horror,
Went a murmur of resistance;
But it whispered, bending downward,
"Take my boughs, O Hiawatha!"
    Down he hewed the boughs of cedar,
Shaped them straightway to a frame-work,
Like two bows he formed and shaped them,
Like two bended bows together.
    "Give me of your roots, O Tamarack!
Of your fibrous roots, O Larch-tree!
My canoe to bind together,
So to bind the ends together
That the water may not enter,
That the river may not wet me!"

And the Larch, with all its fibres,
Shivered in the air of morning,
Touched his forehead with its tassels,
Said, with one long sigh of sorrow,
"Take them all, O Hiawatha!"
     From the earth he tore the fibres,
Tore the tough roots of the Larch-tree,
Closely sewed the bark together,
Bound it closely to the frame-work.
     "Give me of your balm, O Fir-tree!
Of your balsam and your resin,
So to close the seams together
That the water may not enter,
That the river may not wet me!"
     And the Fir-tree, tall and sombre,
Sobbed through all its robes of darkness,
Rattled like a shore with pebbles,
Answered wailing, answered weeping,
"Take my balm, O Hiawatha!"
     And he took the tears of balsam,
Took the resin of the Fir-tree,
Smeared therewith each seam and fissure,
Made each crevice safe from water.
     "Give me of your quills, O Hedgehog!
All your quills, O Kagh, the Hedgehog!
I will make a necklace of them,
Make a girdle for my beauty,
And two stars to deck her bosom!"
     From a hollow tree the Hedgehog
With his sleepy eyes looked at him,

Shot his shining quills, like arrows,
Saying with a drowsy murmur,
Through the tangle of his whiskers,
"Take my quills, O Hiawatha!"
    From the ground the quills he gathered,
All the little shining arrows,
Stained them red and blue and yellow,
With the juice of roots and berries;
Into his canoe he wrought them,
Round its waist a shining girdle,
Round its bows a gleaming necklace,
On its breast two stars resplendent.
    Thus the Birch Canoe was builded
In the valley, by the river,
In the bosom of the forest;
And the forest's life was in it,
All its mystery and its magic,
All the lightness of the birch-tree,
All the toughness of the cedar,
All the larch's supple sinews;
And it floated on the river
Like a yellow leaf in Autumn,
Like a yellow water-lily.
    Paddles none had Hiawatha,
Paddles none he had or needed,
For his thoughts as paddles served him,
And his wishes served to guide him;
Swift or slow at will he glided,
Veered to right or left at pleasure.
    Then he called aloud to Kwasind,

To his friend, the strong man, Kwasind,
Saying, "Help me clear this river
Of its sunken logs and sand-bars."
  Straight into the river Kwasind
Plunged as if he were an otter,
Dived as if he were a beaver,
Stood up to his waist in water,
To his arm-pits in the river,
Swam and shouted in the river,
Tugged at sunken logs and branches,
With his hands he scooped the sand-bars,
With his feet the ooze and tangle.
  And thus sailed my Hiawatha
Down the rushing Taquamenaw,
Sailed through all its bends and windings,
Sailed through all its deeps and shallows,
While his friend, the strong man, Kwasind,
Swam the deeps, the shallows waded.
  Up and down the river went they,
In and out among its islands,
Cleared its bed of root and sand-bar,
Dragged the dead trees from its channel,
Made its passage safe and certain,
Made a pathway for the people,
From its springs among the mountains,
To the waters of Pauwating,
To the bay of Taquamenaw.

HIAWATHA'S FISHING

Forth upon the Gitchie Gumee,
On the shining Big-Sea-Water,
With his fishing-line of cedar,
Of the twisted bark of cedar,
Forth to catch the sturgeon Nahma,
Mishe-Nahma, King of Fishes,
In his birch canoe exulting
All alone went Hiawatha.
  Through the clear, transparent water
He could see the fishes swimming
Far down in the depths below him;
See the yellow perch, the Sahwa,
Like a sunbeam in the water,
See the Shawgashee, the craw-fish,
Like a spider on the bottom,
On the white and sandy bottom.
  At the stern sat Hiawatha,
With his fishing-line of cedar,
In his plumes the breeze of morning
Played as in the hemlock branches;
On the bows, with tail erected,
Sat the squirrel, Adjidaumo;
In his fur the breeze of morning
Played as in the prairie grasses.

On the white sand of the bottom
Lay the monster Mishe-Nahma,
Lay the sturgeon, King of Fishes;
Through his gills he breathed the water,
With his fins he fanned and winnowed,
With his tail he swept the sand-floor.
   There he lay, in all his armor;
On each side a shield to guard him,
Plates of bone upon his forehead,
Down his sides and back and shoulders
Plates of bone with spines projecting!
Painted was he with his war-paints,
Stripes of yellow, red, and azure.
Spots of brown and spots of sable;
And he lay there on the bottom,
Fanning with his fins of purple,
As above him Hiawatha
In his birch canoe came sailing,
With his fishing-line of cedar.
   "Take my bait," cried Hiawatha,
Down into the depths beneath him,
"Take my bait, O Sturgeon, Nahma!
Come up from below the water,
Let us see which is the stronger!"
And he dropped his line of cedar
Through the clear, transparent water,
Waited vainly for an answer,
Long sat waiting for an answer,
And repeating loud and louder,
"Take my bait, O King of Fishes!"

Quiet lay the sturgeon, Nahma,
Fanning slowly in the water,
Looking up at Hiawatha,
Listening to his call and clamor,
His unnecessary tumult,
Till he wearied of the shouting;
And he said to the Kenozha,
To the pike, the Maskenozha,
"Take the bait of this rude fellow,
Break the line of Hiawatha!"

In his fingers Hiawatha
Felt the loose line jerk and tighten;
As he drew it in, it tugged so
That the birch canoe stood endwise,
Like a birch log in the water,
With the squirrel, Adjidaumo,
Perched and frisking on the summit.

Full of scorn was Hiawatha
When he saw the fish rise upward,
Saw the pike, the Maskenozha,
Coming nearer, nearer to him,
And he shouted through the water,
"Esa! esa! shame upon you!
You are but the pike, Kenozha,
You are not the fish I wanted,
You are not the King of Fishes!"

Reeling downward to the bottom
Sank the pike in great confusion,
And the mighty sturgeon, Nahma,
Said to Ugudwash, the sun-fish,

To the bream, with scales of crimson,
"Take the bait of this great boaster,
Break the line of Hiawatha!"

Slowly upward, wavering, gleaming,
Rose the Ugudwash, the sun-fish,
Seized the line of Hiawatha,
Swung with all his weight upon it,
Made a whirlpool in the water,
Whirled the birch canoe in circles,
Round and round in gurgling eddies,
Till the circles in the water
Reached the far-off sandy beaches,
Till the water-flags and rushes
Nodded on the distant margins.

But when Hiawatha saw him
Slowly rising through the water,
Lifting up his disk refulgent,
Loud he shouted in derision,
"Esa! esa! shame upon you!
You are Ugudwash, the sun-fish,
You are not the fish I wanted,
You are not the King of Fishes!"

Slowly downward, wavering, gleaming,
Sank the Ugudwash, the sun-fish,
And again the sturgeon, Nahma,
Heard the shout of Hiawatha,
Heard his challenge of defiance,
The unnecessary tumult,
Ringing far across the water.

From the white sand of the bottom

Up he rose with angry gesture,
Quivering in each nerve and fibre,
Clashing all his plates of armor,
Gleaming bright with all his war-paint;
In his wrath he darted upward,
Flashing leaped into the sunshine,
Opened his great jaws, and swallowed
Both canoe and Hiawatha.

Down into that darksome cavern
Plunged the headlong Hiawatha,
As a log on some black river
Shoots and plunges down the rapids,
Found himself in utter darkness,
Groped about in helpless wonder,
Till he felt a great heart beating,
Throbbing in that utter darkness.

And he smote it in his anger,
With his fist, the heart of Nahma.
Felt the mighty King of Fishes
Shudder through each nerve and fibre,
Heard the water gurgle round him
As he leaped and staggered through it,
Sick at heart, and faint and weary.

Crosswise then did Hiawatha
Drag his birch-canoe for safety,
Lest from out the jaws of Nahma,
In the turmoil and confusion,
Forth he might be hurled and perish,
And the squirrel, Adjidaumo,
Frisked and chattered very gayly,

Toiled and tugged with Hiawatha
Till the labor was completed.
  Then said Hiawatha to him,
"O my little friend, the squirrel,
Bravely have you toiled to help me;
Take the thanks of Hiawatha,
And the name which now he gives you;
For hereafter and forever
Boys shall call you Adjidaumo,
Tail-in-air the boys shall call you!"
  And again the sturgeon, Nahma,
Gasped and quivered in the water,
Then was still, and drifted landward
Till he grated on the pebbles,
Till the listening Hiawatha
Heard him grate upon the margin,
Felt him strand upon the pebbles,
Knew that Nahma, King of Fishes,
Lay there dead upon the margin.
  Then he heard a clang and flapping,
As of many wings assembling,
Heard a screaming and confusion,
As of birds of prey contending,
Saw a gleam of light above him,
Shining through the ribs of Nahma,
Saw the glittering eyes of sea-gulls,
Of Kayoshk, the sea-gulls, peering,
Gazing at him through the opening,
Heard them saying to each other,

"'T is our brother, Hiawatha!"
    And he shouted from below them,
Cried exulting from the caverns:
"O ye sea-gulls! O my brothers!
I have slain the sturgeon, Nahma;
Make the rifts a little larger,
With your claws the openings widen,
Set me free from this dark prison,
And henceforward and forever
Men shall speak of your achievements,
Calling you Kayoshk, the sea-gulls,
Yes, Kayoshk, the Noble Scratchers!"
    And the wild and clamorous sea-gulls
Toiled with beak and claws together,
Made the rifts and openings wider
In the mighty ribs of Nahma,
And from peril and from prison,
From the body of the sturgeon,
From the peril of the water,
They released my Hiawatha.

    He was standing near his wigwam,
On the margin of the water,
And he called to old Nokomis,
Called and beckoned to Nokomis,
Pointed to the sturgeon, Nahma,
Lying lifeless on the pebbles,
With the sea-gulls feeding on him.
    "I have slain the Mishe-Nahma,
Slain the King of Fishes!" said he;

"Look! the sea-gulls feed upon him,
Yes, my friends Kayoshk, the sea-gulls;
Drive them not away, Nokomis,
They have saved me from great peril
In the body of the sturgeon,
Wait until their meal is ended,
Till their craws are full with feasting,
Till they homeward fly, at sunset,
To their nests among the marshes;
Then bring all your pots and kettles,
And make oil for us in Winter."

And she waited till the sun set,
Till the pallid moon, the Night-sun,
Rose above the tranquil water,
Till Kayoshk, the sated sea-gulls,
From their banquet rose with clamor,
And across the fiery sunset
Winged their way to far-off islands,
To their nests among the rushes.

To his sleep went Hiawatha,
And Nokomis to her labor,
Toiling patient in the moonlight,
Till the sun and moon changed places,
Till the sky was red with sunrise,
And Kayoshk, the hungry sea-gulls,
Came back from the reedy islands,
Clamorous for their morning banquet.

Three whole days and nights alternate
Old Nokomis and the sea-gulls

Stripped the oily flesh of Nahma,
Till the waves washed through the rib-bones,
Till the sea-gulls came no longer,
And upon the sands lay nothing
But the skeleton of Nahma.

THE BUILDING OF THE SHIP

"Build me straight, O worthy Master!
  Stanch and strong, a goodly vessel,
That shall laugh at all disaster,
  And with wave and whirlwind wrestle!"

The merchant's word
Delighted the Master heard;
For his heart was in his work, and the heart
Giveth grace unto every Art.
A quiet smile played round his lips,
As the eddies and dimples of the tide
Play round the bows of ships,
That steadily at anchor ride.
And with a voice that was full of glee,
He answered, "Erelong we will launch
A vessel as goodly, and strong, and stanch,
As ever weathered a wintry sea!"
And first with nicest skill and art,
Perfect and finished in every part,
A little model the Master wrought,
Which should be to the larger plan
What the child is to the man,
Its counterpart in miniature;
That with a hand more swift and sure
The greater labor might be brought
To answer to his inward thought.

And as he labored, his mind ran o'er
The various ships that were built of yore,
And above them all, and strangest of all
Towered the Great Harry, crank and tall,
Whose picture was hanging on the wall,
With bows and stern raised high in air,
And balconies hanging here and there,
And signal lanterns and flags afloat,
And eight round towers, like those that frown
From some old castle, looking down
Upon the drawbridge and the moat.
And he said with a smile, "Our ship, I wis,
Shall be of another form than this!"
It was of another form, indeed;
Built for freight, and yet for speed,
A beautiful and gallant craft;
Broad in the beam, that the stress of the blast,
Pressing down upon sail and mast,
Might not the sharp bows overwhelm;
Broad in the beam, but sloping aft
With graceful curve and slow degrees,
That she might be docile to the helm,
And that the currents of parted seas,
Closing behind, with mighty force,
Might aid and not impede her course.
In the ship-yard stood the Master,
With the model of the vessel,
That should laugh at all disaster,
And with wave and whirlwind wrestle!

Covering many a rood of ground,
Lay the timber piled around;
Timber of chestnut, and elm, and oak,
And scattered here and there, with these,
The knarred and crooked cedar knees;
Brought from regions far away,
From Pascagoula's sunny bay,
And the banks of the roaring Roanoke!
Ah! what a wondrous thing it is
To note how many wheels of toil
One thought, one word, can set in motion!
There's not a ship that sails the ocean,
But every climate, every soil,
Must bring its tribute, great or small,
And help to build the wooden wall!

The sun was rising o'er the sea,
And long the level shadows lay,
As if they, too, the beams would be
Of some great, airy argosy,
Framed and launched in a single day.
That silent architect, the sun,
Had hewn and laid them every one,
Ere the work of man was yet begun.
Beside the Master, when he spoke,
A youth, against an anchor leaning,
Listened, to catch his slightest meaning.
Only the long waves, as they broke
In ripples on the pebbly beach,
Interrupted the old man's speech.

Beautiful they were, in sooth,
The old man and the fiery youth!
The old man, in whose busy brain
Many a ship that sailed the main
Was modelled o'er and o'er again;—
The fiery youth, who was to be
The heir of his dexterity,
The heir of his house, and his daughter's hand,
When he had built and launched from land
What the elder head had planned.

"Thus," said he, "will we build this ship!
Lay square the blocks upon the slip,
And follow well this plan of mine.
Choose the timbers with greatest care;
Of all that is unsound beware;
For only what is sound and strong
To this vessel shall belong.
Cedar of Maine and Georgia pine
Here together shall combine.
A goodly frame, and a goodly fame,
And the *Union* be her name!
For the day that gives her to the sea
Shall give my daughter unto thee!"

The Master's word
Enraptured the young man heard;
And as he turned his face aside,
With a look of joy and a thrill of pride,
Standing before

Her father's door,
He saw the form of his promised bride.
The sun shone on her golden hair,
And her cheek was glowing fresh and fair,
With the breath of morn and the soft sea air.
Like a beauteous barge was she,
Still at rest on the sandy beach,
Just beyond the billow's reach;
But he
Was the restless, seething, stormy sea!

Ah, how skilful grows the hand
That obeyeth Love's command!
It is the heart, and not the brain,
That to the highest doth attain,
And he who followeth Love's behest
Far excelleth all the rest!
Thus with the rising of the sun
Was the noble task begun,
And soon throughout the ship-yard's bounds
Were heard the intermingled sounds
Of axes and of mallets, plied
With vigorous arms on every side;
Plied so deftly and so well,
That, ere the shadows of evening fell,
The keel of oak for a noble ship,
Scarfed and bolted, straight and strong,
Was lying ready, and stretched along
The blocks, well placed upon the slip.

Happy, thrice happy, every one
Who sees his labor well begun,
And not perplexed and multiplied,
By idly waiting for time and tide!

And when the hot, long day was o'er,
The young man at the Master's door
Sat with the maiden calm and still,
And within the porch, a little more
Removed beyond the evening chill,
The father sat, and told them tales
Of wrecks in the great September gales,
Of pirates coasting the Spanish Main,
And ships that never came back again,
The chance and change of a sailor's life,
Want and plenty, rest and strife,
His roving fancy, like the wind,
That nothing can stay and nothing can bind,
And the magic charm of foreign lands,
With shadows of palms, and shining sands,
Where the tumbling surf,
O'er the coral reefs of Madagascar,
Washes the feet of the swarthy Lascar,
As he lies alone and asleep on the turf.
And the trembling maiden held her breath
At the tales of that awful, pitiless sea,
With all its terror and mystery,
The dim, dark sea, so like unto Death,
That divides and yet unites mankind!

And whenever the old man paused, a gleam
From the bowl of his pipe would awhile illume
The silent group in the twilight gloom,
And thoughtful faces, as in a dream;
And for a moment one might mark
What had been hidden by the dark,
That the head of the maiden lay at rest,
Tenderly, on the young man's breast!

Day by day the vessel grew,
With timbers fashioned strong and true,
Stemson and keelson and sternson-knee,
Till, framed with perfect symmetry,
A skeleton ship rose up to view!
And around the bows and along the side
The heavy hammers and mallets plied,
Till after many a week, at length,
Wonderful for form and strength,
Sublime in its enormous bulk,
Loomed aloft the shadowy hulk!
And around it columns of smoke, upwreathing,
Rose from the boiling, bubbling, seething
Caldron, that glowed,
And overflowed
With the black tar, heated for the sheathing.
And amid the clamors
Of clattering hammers,
He who listened heard now and then
The song of the Master and his men:—

"Build me straight, O worthy Master,
   Stanch and strong, a goodly vessel,
That shall laugh at all disaster,
   And with wave and whirlwind wrestle!"

With oaken brace and copper band,
Lay the rudder on the sand,
That, like a thought, should have control
Over the movement of the whole;
And near it the anchor, whose giant hand
Would reach down and grapple with the land,
And immovable and fast
Hold the great ship against the bellowing blast!
And at the bows an image stood,
By a cunning artist carved in wood,
With robes of white, that far behind
Seemed to be fluttering in the wind.
It was not shaped in a classic mould,
Not like a Nymph or Goddess of old,
Or Naiad rising from the water,
But modelled from the Master's daughter!
On many a dreary and misty night,
'T will be seen by the rays of the signal light,
Speeding along through the rain and the dark,
Like a ghost in its snow-white sark,
The pilot of some phantom bark,
Guiding the vessel, in its flight,
By a path none other knows aright!

Behold, at last,
Each tall and tapering mast
Is swung into its place;
Shrouds and stays
Holding it firm and fast!

Long ago,
In the deer-haunted forests of Maine,
When upon mountain and plain
Lay the snow,
They fell, — those lordly pines!
Those grand, majestic pines!
'Mid shouts and cheers
The jaded steers,
Panting beneath the goad,
Dragged down the weary, winding road
Those captive kings so straight and tall,
To be shorn of their streaming hair,
And naked and bare,
To feel the stress and the strain
Of the wind and the reeling main,
Whose roar
Would remind them forevermore
Of their native forests they should not see again.

And everywhere
The slender, graceful spars
Poise aloft in the air,
And at the mast-head,
White, blue, and red,

A flag unrolls the stripes and stars.
Ah! when the wanderer, lonely, friendless,
In foreign harbors shall behold
That flag unrolled,
'T will be as a friendly hand
Stretched out from his native land,
Filling his heart with memories sweet and endless!

All is finished! and at length
Has come the bridal day
Of beauty and of strength.
To-day the vessel shall be launched!
With fleecy clouds the sky is blanched,
And o'er the bay,
Slowly, in all its splendors dight,
The great sun rises to behold the sight.

The ocean old,
Centuries old,
Strong as youth, and as uncontrolled,
Paces restless to and fro,
Up and down the sands of gold.
His beating heart is not at rest;
And far and wide,
With ceaseless flow,
His beard of snow
Heaves with the heaving of his breast.
He waits impatient for his bride.
There she stands,
With her foot upon the sands,

Decked with flags and streamers gay,
In honor of her marriage day,
Her snow-white signals fluttering, blending,
Round her like a veil descending,
Ready to be
The bride of the gray old sea.

On the deck another bride
Is standing by her lover's side.
Shadows from the flags and shrouds,
Like the shadows cast by clouds,
Broken by many a sudden fleck,
Fall around them on the deck.
The prayer is said,
The service read,
The joyous bridegroom bows his head;
And in tears the good old Master
Shakes the brown hand of his son,
Kisses his daughter's glowing cheek
In silence, for he cannot speak,
And ever faster
Down his own the tears begin to run.
The worthy pastor—
The shepherd of that wandering flock,
That has the ocean for its wold,
That has the vessel for its fold,
Leaping ever from rock to rock—
Spake, with accents mild and clear,
Words of warning, words of cheer,

But tedious to the bridegroom's ear.
He knew the chart
Of the sailor's heart,
All its pleasures and its griefs,
All its shallows and rocky reefs,
All those secret currents, that flow
With such resistless undertow,
And lift and drift, with terrible force,
The will from its moorings and its course.
Therefore he spake, and thus said he:—
"Like unto ships far off at sea,
Outward or homeward bound, are we.
Before, behind, and all around,
Floats and swings the horizon's bound,
Seems at its distant rim to rise
And climb the crystal wall of the skies,
And then again to turn and sink,
As if we could slide from its outer brink.
Ah! it is not the sea,
It is not the sea that sinks and shelves,
But ourselves
That rock and rise
With endless and uneasy motion,
Now touching the very skies,
Now sinking into the depths of ocean.
Ah! if our souls but poise and swing
Like the compass in its brazen ring,
Ever level and ever true
To the toil and the task we have to do,

We shall sail securely, and safely reach
The Fortunate Isles, on whose shining beach
The sights we see, and the sounds we hear,
Will be those of joy and not of fear!"

Then the Master,
With a gesture of command,
Waved his hand;
And at the word,
Loud and sudden there was heard,
All around them and below,
The sound of hammers, blow on blow,
Knocking away the shores and spurs.
And see! she stirs!
She starts, — she moves, — she seems to feel
The thrill of life along her keel,
And, spurning with her foot the ground,
With one exulting, joyous bound,
She leaps into the ocean's arms!

And lo! from the assembled crowd
There rose a shout, prolonged and loud,
That to the ocean seemed to say,
"Take her, O bridegroom, old and gray,
Take her to thy protecting arms,
With all her youth and all her charms!"

How beautiful she is! How fair
She lies within those arms, that press
Her form with many a soft caress

Of tenderness and watchful care!
Sail forth into the sea, O ship!
Through wind and wave, right onward steer!
The moistened eye, the trembling lip,
Are not the signs of doubt or fear.

Sail forth into the sea of life,
O gentle, loving, trusting wife,
And safe from all adversity
Upon the bosom of that sea
Thy comings and thy goings be!
For gentleness and love and trust
Prevail o'er angry wave and gust;
And in the wreck of noble lives
Something immortal still survives!

Thou, too, sail on, O Ship of State!
Sail on, O *Union,* strong and great!
Humanity with all its fears,
With all the hopes of future years,
Is hanging breathless on thy fate!
We know what Master laid thy keel,
What Workmen wrought thy ribs of steel,
Who made each mast, and sail, and rope,
What anvils rang, what hammers beat,
In what a forge and what a heat
Were shaped the anchors of thy hope!
Fear not each sudden sound and shock,
'T is of the wave and not the rock;
'T is but the flapping of the sail,

And not a rent made by the gale!
In spite of rock and tempest's roar,
In spite of false lights on the shore,
Sail on, nor fear to breast the sea!
Our hearts, our hopes, are all with thee,
Our hearts, our hopes, our prayers, our tears,
Our faith triumphant o'er our fears,
Are all with thee,—are all with thee!

Olive Rush

THE CASTLE-BUILDER

A gentle boy, with soft and silken locks,
    A dreamy boy, with brown and tender eyes,
A castle-builder, with his wooden blocks,
    And towers that touch imaginary skies.

A fearless rider on his father's knee,
    An eager listener unto stories told
At the Round Table of the nursery,
    Of heroes and adventures manifold.

There will be other towers for thee to build;
    There will be other steeds for thee to ride;
There will be other legends, and all filled
    With greater marvels and more glorified.

Build on, and make thy castles high and fair,
    Rising and reaching upward to the skies;
Listening to voices in the upper air,
    Nor lose thy simple faith in mysteries.

PAUL REVERE'S RIDE

Listen, my children, and you shall hear
Of the midnight ride of Paul Revere,
On the eighteenth of April, in Seventy-five;
Hardly a man is now alive
Who remembers that famous day and year.

He said to his friend, "If the British march
By land or sea from the town to-night,
Hang a lantern aloft in the belfry-arch
Of the North Church tower as a signal light, —
One, if by land, and two, if by sea;
And I on the opposite shore will be,
Ready to ride and spread the alarm
Through every Middlesex village and farm,
For the country folk to be up and to arm."

Then he said, "Good night!" and with muffled oar
Silently rowed to the Charlestown shore,
Just as the moon rose over the bay,
Where swinging wide at her moorings lay
The Somerset, British man-of-war;
A phantom ship, with each mast and spar
Across the moon like a prison bar,
And a huge black hulk, that was magnified
By its own reflection in the tide.

Meanwhile, his friend, through alley and street,
Wanders and watches with eager ears,
Till in the silence around him he hears
The muster of men at the barrack door,
The sound of arms, and the tramp of feet,
And the measured tread of the grenadiers,
Marching down to their boats on the shore.

Then he climbed the tower of the Old North Church,
By the wooden stairs, with stealthy tread,
To the belfry-chamber overhead,
And startled the pigeons from their perch
On the sombre rafters, that round him made
Masses and moving shapes of shade, —
By the trembling ladder, steep and tall,
To the highest window in the wall,
Where he paused to listen and look down
A moment on the roofs of the town,
And the moonlight flowing over all.

Beneath, in the churchyard, lay the dead,
In their night-encampment on the hill,
Wrapped in silence so deep and still
That he could hear, like a sentinel's tread,
The watchful night-wind, as it went
Creeping along from tent to tent,
And seeming to whisper, "All is well!"
A moment only he feels the spell

Of the place and the hour, and the secret dread
Of the lonely belfry and the dead;
For suddenly all his thoughts are bent
On a shadowy something far away,
Where the river widens to meet the bay, —
A line of black that bends and floats
On the rising tide, like a bridge of boats.

Meanwhile, impatient to mount and ride,
Booted and spurred, with a heavy stride
On the opposite shore walked Paul Revere.
Now he patted his horse's side,
Now gazed at the landscape far and near,
Then, impetuous, stamped the earth,
And turned and tightened his saddle-girth;
But mostly he watched with eager search
The belfry-tower of the Old North Church,
As it rose above the graves on the hill,
Lonely and spectral and sombre and still.
And lo! as he looks, on the belfry's height
A glimmer, and then a gleam of light!
He springs to the saddle, the bridle he turns,
But lingers and gazes, till full on his sight,
A second lamp in the belfry burns!
A hurry of hoofs in a village street,
A shape in the moonlight, a bulk in the dark,
And beneath, from the pebbles, in passing, a spark
Struck out by a steed flying fearless and fleet:
That was all! And yet, through the gloom and the light,
The fate of a nation was riding that night;

And the spark struck out by that steed, in his flight,
Kindled the land into flame with its heat.

He has left the village and mounted the steep,
And beneath him, tranquil and broad and deep,
Is the Mystic, meeting the ocean tides;
And under the alders that skirt its edge,
Now soft on the sand, now loud on the ledge,
Is heard the tramp of his steed as he rides.

It was twelve by the village clock,
When he crossed the bridge into Medford town.
He heard the crowing of the cock,
And the barking of the farmer's dog,
And felt the damp of the river fog,
That rises after the sun goes down.

It was one by the village clock,
When he galloped into Lexington.
He saw the gilded weathercock
Swim in the moonlight as he passed,
And the meeting-house windows, blank and bare,
Gaze at him with a spectral glare,
As if they already stood aghast
At the bloody work they would look upon.

It was two by the village clock,
When he came to the bridge in Concord town
He heard the bleating of the flock,
And the twitter of birds among the trees,

And felt the breath of the morning breeze
Blowing over the meadows brown.
And one was safe and asleep in his bed
Who at the bridge would be first to fall,
Who that day would be lying dead,
Pierced by a British musket-ball.

You know the rest. In the books you have read,
How the British Regulars fired and fled, —
How the farmers gave them ball for ball,
From behind each fence and farm-yard wall,
Chasing the red-coats down the lane,
Then crossing the fields to emerge again
Under the trees at the turn of the road,
And only pausing to fire and load.

So through the night rode Paul Revere;
And so through the night went his cry of alarm
To every Middlesex village and farm, —
A cry of defiance and not of fear,
A voice in the darkness, a knock at the door,
And a word that shall echo forevermore!
For, borne on the night-wind of the Past,
Through all our history, to the last,
In the hour of darkness and peril and need,
The people will waken and listen to hear
The hurrying hoof-beats of that steed
And the midnight message of Paul Revere.

THE BUILDING OF THE LONG SERPENT

Thorberg Skafting, master-builder,
   In his ship-yard by the sea,
Whistling, said, "It would bewilder
Any man but Thorberg Skafting,
   Any man but me!"

Near him lay the Dragon stranded,
   Built of old by Raud the Strong,
And King Olaf had commanded
He should build another Dragon,
   Twice as large and long.

Therefore whistled Thorberg Skafting,
   As he sat with half-closed eyes,
And his head turned sideways, drafting
That new vessel for King Olaf
   Twice the Dragon's size.

Round him busily hewed and hammered
   Mallet huge and heavy axe;
Workmen laughed and sang and clamored;
Whirred the wheels, that into rigging
   Spun the shining flax!

All this tumult heard the master, —
    It was music to his ear;
Fancy whispered all the faster,
"Men shall hear of Thorberg Skafting
    For a hundred year!"

Workmen sweating at the forges
    Fashioned iron bolt and bar,
Like a warlock's midnight orgies
Smoked and bubbled the black caldron
    With the boiling tar.

Did the warlocks mingle in it,
    Thorberg Skafting, any curse?
Could you not be gone a minute
But some mischief must be doing,
    Turning bad to worse?

'T was an ill wind that came wafting
    From his homestead words of woe;
To his farm went Thorberg Skafting,
Oft repeating to his workmen,
    Build ye thus and so.

After long delays returning
    Came the master back by night;
To his ship-yard longing, yearning,
Hurried he, and did not leave it
    Till the morning's light.

"Come and see my ship, my darling!"
    On the morrow said the King;
"Finished now from keel to carling;
Never yet was seen in Norway
    Such a wondrous thing!"

In the ship-yard, idly talking,
    At the ship the workmen stared:
Some one, all their labor balking,
Down her sides had cut deep gashes,
    Not a plank was spared!

"Death be to the evil-doer!"
    With an oath King Olaf spoke!
"But rewards to his pursuer!"
And with wrath his face grew redder
    Than his scarlet cloak.

Straight the master-builder, smiling,
    Answered thus the angry King:
"Cease blaspheming and reviling
Olaf, it was Thorberg Skafting
    Who has done this thing!"

Then he chipped and smoothed the planking,
    Till the King, delighted, swore,
With much lauding and much thanking,
"Handsomer is now my Dragon
    Than she was before!"

Seventy ells and four extended
   On the grass the vessel's keel;
High above it, gilt and splendid,
Rose the figure-head ferocious
   With its crest of steel.

Then they launched her from the tressels,
   In the ship-yard by the sea;
She was the grandest of all vessels,
Never ship was built in Norway
   Half so fine as she!

The Long Serpent was she christened,
   'Mid the roar of cheer on cheer!
They who to the Saga listened
Heard the name of Thorberg Skafting
   For a hundred year!